ANIMAL PREDATORS

Lions

SANDRA MARKLE

❧ CAROLRHODA BOOKS, INC./ MINNEAPOLIS

THE ANIMAL WORLD IS FULL OF
PREDATORS.

Predators are the hunters who find, catch, and eat other animals—their prey—in order to survive. Every environment has its chain of hunters. The smaller, slower, less able predators become prey for the bigger, faster, more cunning hunters. And everywhere, there are just a few kinds of predators at the top of the food chain. *In the African grasslands, one of these is the lion.*

Why are lions such good hunters? For one thing, a lion has sharp senses to help it find prey. A lion's nose may bring the first clue that prey is nearby. Sniffing the air brings scents to chemical-sensitive sensors in the lion's nasal passages. Even if a lion doesn't smell prey, it may hear it. A lion's two ears can turn in different directions at the same time to pick up sounds that guide it to prey. But a lion depends most on its eyesight. Big eyes give the lion a broad view of the world around it. And because its two eyes face forward, a lion can easily judge the distance between itself and its prey. Knowing the distance is important for deciding when to pounce.

Of course, prey animals, such as these Cape buffalo, are always on the alert for lions. Cape buffalo live in herds, or groups, of animals. A herd has many eyes and ears checking for lions. This Cape buffalo, with eyes and ears high on its head, is watching and listening all around itself even while it's getting a drink of water.

Lions are successful hunters because they're also part of a group, called a pride. Lions use teamwork to catch prey. Usually it's the lionesses, the female members of the pride, who do the hunting. This group sets off late in the afternoon as the sun sinks low in the sky. The lionesses lope along close together, heads up, listening and watching.

The males sometimes help kill big game, such as a wildebeest. Mainly, though, they patrol their pride's hunting territory to drive off wandering males hunting alone or groups of lionesses. When patrolling, males mark the pride's claim to their home range by roaring and by spraying urine on rocks or bushes to leave their scent. Having a home range is important to the pride, ensuring that the lions are able to catch food without having to travel long distances.

Lions are clever hunters. The first lioness to spot the group of grazing Cape buffalo gives a throaty huff and lowers her belly close to the ground. The others quickly follow, and their tawny-colored bodies disappear into the dry grass.

Staying low as they stalk and freezing every few paces, the lionesses slip closer to the herd. Next, the hunters split up. Some of the lionesses move into the open to attract attention. When the herd of buffalo sees them, it bellows a warning and turns to face the lionesses. A Cape buffalo defends itself with its sharp horns and hooves.

Meanwhile, two lionesses slip up behind the herd. Lions have their own set of weapons: strong muscles, long claws, and sharp teeth. Suddenly, like releasing a stretched rubber band, one lioness's powerful leg muscles launch her forward. An instant later, her partner springs too.

Lions depend on their sharp claws to catch prey. While she was running, the lioness's claws were retracted, or pulled into her paws, to protect them. Now, as she grabs a buffalo's rump, stretchy cords called tendons push the lioness's toe tips downward, thrusting out the needle-sharp claws.

The captured bull bellows, struggling to pull free. The rest of the buffalo herd flees, thundering away as the other lionesses join in the attack. Two leap onto the buffalo's back. Their combined weight holds down the bull for a few seconds. Then he staggers to his feet, knocking the lionesses off. One hunter charges the bull's head but backs off to avoid being kicked.

The struggle continues for more than an hour. Finally, one of the lionesses clamps her mouth over the buffalo's nose and mouth, cutting off his air supply. Within minutes, the buffalo is dead.

After the prey is killed, the lionesses no longer work as a team. They snarl and bump shoulders, competing to claim the favorite parts of the kill—the heart, liver, and lungs. The lionesses' roars bring the pride's males and cubs to the kill. The adult males move in to claim their share. They tear into the buffalo's rump, peeling meat off the bone with their rough tongues.

One cub gets too close to a male and is swatted away. The lionesses lead their cubs away to wait until the males finish. Then the lionesses and the cubs take their place at the kill, gnawing the scraps off the bones.

Once the pride finishes eating, it's time to clean up. A lion's tongue, covered with backward-curving spines, makes a natural comb. Besides cleaning away blood and dirt, licking spreads oil produced in the lion's skin onto its fur. This helps the big cat shed water and stay warm when it rains. Group grooming also strengthens the pride's sense of family.

Then it's time for the cubs to nurse. Their mother's milk adds to their diet, helping the cubs grow big and strong. The cubs continue to nurse for about eight months. It's not unusual for lionesses with cubs to share nursing each other's offspring.

Next, the lions stretch out to sleep. The lions spend most of the time they aren't hunting asleep—as much as eighteen hours a day. Sleeping is a good way to save up energy for the next hunt. A short nap is enough for the cubs, though. So they start to play.

The cubs wrestle until their mother wakes up. When she growls in irritation, the cubs go off to investigate their surroundings.

Everything intrigues lion cubs. They sniff at a hole and paw at a tortoise until it retreats inside its shell. One cub discovers the remains of an antelope and drags it between its legs in the same way it will one day move prey to a shady feeding spot. Day after day, the cubs play at hunting, building their skills, and muscle strength. By the time they're two, the young lions are already catching small game, like hares and foxes.

When it comes to hunting bigger prey, though, the young lions still have a lot to learn. They're likely to stay clustered together when they could be more successful if they spread out.

They're also likely to charge before they get close enough to strike, giving fast prey, like giraffes, time to escape. Each lost meal is a valuable hunting lesson.

The young lions also develop their skills by hunting with the pride. When they hunt at night, the youngsters learn an important lesson—hearing is more important than seeing until the prey is close. When the prey is nearer, lions can see it even in dim moonlight. That's because they have a mirrorlike layer at the back of their eyes. This reflects light that enters the eyes back onto the light-sensitive cells that send messages to the brain. Increasing the number of messages the brain receives from the eye sharpens the image the lion sees.

Walking through tall grass in the soft evening light, one of the young lions startles a warthog. Snorting, the warthog leaps up. One of the lionesses runs after it and swipes the warthog's back legs, knocking it down. The reward of fresh meat reinforces this hunting strategy.

Africa is a land of two seasons—dry and wet. As in countless years past, the arrival of the rains settles the dust and gives life to seeds waiting to sprout. Soon the humid air carries flower scents. Rocky riverbeds disappear beneath flowing water, and when the new grass sprouts, herds of zebras and other animals arrive to graze. With so many big prey animals available, the young lions finally have a chance to perfect their hunting skills.

The pride of lionesses lopes along with the hunters-in-training bringing up the rear. The lions hear and smell the zebra herd even before they see them. When one of the lionesses huffs a warning, the big cats all drop on their bellies. Tall tussocks of dry grass give the lions cover. Just ahead is a small group of zebras that has wandered away from the main herd. The zebras plod along single file while the hunters slip closer.

When the wind shifts, several of the zebras catch the lions' scent. The zebras swing toward the hunters, barking a warning cry. Quickly the zebras line up to face the lions. The zebras are ready to defend themselves with their hooves and teeth. However, while the zebras watch the lionesses they can see, some of the young hunters slip up behind the herd. Suddenly, spotting them, the zebras bolt.

A young lion singles out one of the zebras and chases after it. The young lion's padded feet push hard against the dirt as it runs in the zebra's dusty wake. The lion's eyes stay locked on its target so when the zebra swerves it turns too. The lion's long tail helps keep the hunter balanced as it strains to gain on the zebra. Hunter and prey are running flat out. Each is running for its life.

Finally, the lion gets close enough to swipe the zebra's hind legs.

When the zebra crashes to the ground, the other lions rush to join in the attack. One of the lionesses holds down the zebra. Then one of the young hunters dives for the prey's throat and locks on. While this young hunter makes the kill, the other members of the pride start competing for the best places to feed. Their roars signal the males to join in.

This is the first of many kills the young lions will share with their pride. The hunting family is now one generation stronger.

Looking Back

- Look at the whiskers on the lion on the cover. When touched, these stiff hairs on either side of its nose send signals to the cat's brain, helping it judge how close things are. When it pounces, the lion pulls its whiskers forward to help it judge when to sink its teeth into its prey.

- Take another look at the Cape buffalo on page 6. Can you guess why it helps the animal to have its horns form a band across the top of its head?

- Check out the lion's long claws on page 13. Just like human fingernails, the claws keep growing. Why would that be important for the hunter?

- On page 19, look at the lion's teeth. Unlike your teeth, which are a mix of pointed and flat, all of a lion's teeth are pointed and sharp. Instead of chewing its food, a lion just slices off chunks of meat and swallows.

- Look at the zebras on page 29. You can see how their stripes help protect zebras by making it harder for a predator to pick a single animal out of the herd.

Glossary

CUB: a young lion

EAR: a body part that detects sound vibrations

EYE: a body part that detects reflected light rays

HERD: a group of the same kind of animal that lives, feeds, and travels together

HOME RANGE: the area within which an animal usually hunts

LIONESS: a female lion

PREDATOR: an animal that hunts other animals

PREY: an animal that a predator catches to eat

PRIDE: a group of lions that live and hunt together

ROAR: the loud, growling noise a lion makes

TONGUE: a bundle of movable muscles inside the mouth. A lion's tongue is covered with hooks that it uses to scrape meat off bones, to carry water and blood into its mouth, and to clean its fur.

Further Information

BOOKS

Darling, Kathy. *Lions.* Minneapolis: Lerner Publications Company, 2000. This book has information about lion societies and life cycles.

Denis-Huot, Christine, and Michel Denis-Huot. *The Lion: King of the Beasts.* Watertown, MA: Charlesbridge Publishing, 2000. Gain insights into a lion's life, especially how each individual is an important part of a social group.

Kaiman, Bobbie, and Amanda Bishop. *Life Cycle of a Lion.* New York: Crabtree Publishing Company, 2002. Learn about how lions are especially adapted for success in their natural habitat.

Markle, Sandra. *Outside and Inside Big Cats.* New York: Atheneum, 2003. Learn how the parts of lions and tigers work together to help the animals live and reproduce.

Winner, Cherie. *Lions.* Chanhassen, MN: NorthWord Press, 2001. This book is packed with fun facts about lions.

VIDEOS

Born Free (Columbia/Tristar Studios, 1966). Learn the true story of Elsa the lion and how the Adamsons reintroduced her into the wild.

National Geographic's Eternal Enemies: Lions and Hyenas (National Geographic, 1992). Gain valuable insights into the competition for prey among predators.

National Geographic's Lions of Darkness (National Geographic, 1997). Take an in-depth look at a year in the life of one pride as shown by filmmakers Dereck and Beverly Joubert.

Index

With love, for dear friends, John and Barbara Clampet.

The author would like to thank the following persons for sharing their expertise and enthusiasm: Dr. Thomas G. Curro, D.V.M., M.S., Associate Veterinarian; Henry Doorly Zoo, Omaha, Nebraska; and Dr. Kathy Quigley, D.V.M., Hornocker Wildlife Institute. As always, a special thanks to Skip Jeffery, for his help and support.

Photo Acknowledgments

© Rich Kirchner, pp. 1, 17, 18; © Karl and Kay Amman/Bruce Coleman, pp. 3, 8, 23; © Tom and Pat Leeson, p. 4; © Erwin and Peggy Bauer, pp. 6, 20, 24, 29, 37; © William Ruth/Bruce Coleman, Inc., p. 7; © Mitsuaki Iwago/Minden Pictures, pp. 11, 14, 15, 34; © Fritz Polking/Frank Lane Picture Agency/CORBIS, p. 13; © Frans Lanting/Minden Pictures, p.16; © Gerald Lacz/Animals Animals, p. 19; © Joe McDonald/Bruce Coleman, Inc., p. 22; © Rob Nunnington/Oxford Scientific Films, p. 27; © J&D Bartlett/Bruce Coleman, Inc., p. 30; © ABPL/Gerald Hinde/Animals Animals, p. 33; © Erwin and Peggy Bauer/Bruce Coleman, Inc., p. 36.
Cover: © Mitsuaki Iwago/Minden Pictures.
Back cover: © Joe McDonald/Bruce Coleman Inc.

Carolrhoda Books
A division of Lerner Publishing Group
241 First Avenue North
Minneapolis, MN 55401

Website address: www.lernerbooks.com

Library of Congress Cataloging-in-Publication Data

Markle, Sandra.
    Lions / by Sandra Markle.
        p.   cm.—(Animal predators)
    Summary: An introduction to the lives of lions which focuses on how they hunt and how they raise their cubs.
    Includes index.
    ISBN: 1—57505—727—1 (lib. bdg. : alk. paper)
    ISBN: 1—57505—744—7 (pbk. : alk. paper)
    1. Lions—Juvenile literature. [1. Lions.] I. Title.
QL737.C23M2724 2005
599.757—dc21   2003011198

Manufactured in the United States of America
1 2 3 4 5 6 — DP — 10 09 08 07 06 05